WHY STEVE WAS LATE

101 EXCEPTIONAL EXCUSES FOR TERRIBLE TIMEKEEPING

Dave Skinner is a comedy writer, actor and comedian who has worked with, amongst others, Rob Brydon, Steve Coogan, Reeves & Mortimer and Armando Iannucci. His other books include *A Snowflake's Guide to Christmas* and the children's title *There's a Lion in the Library!*

Henry Paker is a comedian and illustrator. Henry co-writes the Radio Academy Award-nominated sitcom *ReincarNathan* and wrote and starred in four series of the sketch show *Small Scenes* (BBC Radio 4). Other books Henry has illustrated include *Kay's Anatomy* and *Don't Arm Wrestle a Pirate*.

WHY STEVE WAS LATE

101 EXCEPTIONAL EXCUSES FOR TERRIBLE TIMEKEEPING

DAVE SKINNER AND HENRY PAKER

Atlantic Books
London

First published in hardback in Great Britain in 2009 by
Atlantic Books, an imprint of Atlantic Books Ltd.

This hardback edition published in Great Britain in 2020
by Atlantic Books

10 9 8 7 6 5 4 3 2 1

A CIP catalogue record for this book is available from the
British Library.

Hardback ISBN: 978 1 83895 161 0
Ebook ISBN: 978 1 84887 435 0

Printed in Italy by ✺ Grafica Veneta SpA

Atlantic Books
An imprint of Atlantic Books Ltd
Ormond House
26–27 Boswell Street
London WC1N 3JZ

www.atlantic-books.co.uk

With thanks to:
Yakup and Ruth Paker,
Geoff and Inez Skinner,
Sally-Anne Johnson,
Sarah Norman, Camilla Hornby
all at Atlantic
and
Matt Peover and Tony Horspool

Meet Steve.

This year Steve was late 101 times.

These are the excuses he gave...

Distracted by a surprisingly complicated Kinder toy

1

Overcome by the urge to alphabetise my pets

Found out I'm adopted

Distracted by world's biggest Sudoku

Forgot how trousers work

7

Accidentally sold myself on eBay

Found God

9

Got stuck in a romantic montage

11

Overwhelmed by the breakfast buffet

Discovered I have an unusual superpower

13

Broke world record for longest ever awkward pause

Bumped into my arch nemesis

15

Family event dragged on

Marooned on a traffic island

17

Discovered I'm jam intolerant

19

Woke up with Magritte Syndrome

21

Turns out it's contagious

Involved in a vending mishap

Departures

PLATFORMS 6-11 →

23

Made an unpopular wallpaper choice

Fell in love with the voice in the Sat Nav

25

Went to the wrong workplace

27

28

Couldn't decide which pen to wear

Got off at the wrong stop

29

Didn't know what to do with my hair

Rubik's Cube took ages in a black and white world

Promised I'd take the kids to Hogwarts

33

Had a falling out with my neighbour

Having trouble with the builders

35

Shouldn't have skipped gym induction

Seduced by the Dark Side

37

38

Saw the error of my ways

Competitive streak got out of hand

Mugged by mime artists

Dental hygienist was more thorough than usual

Had to attend a police line-up

43

Lost a contact lens

Promised I'd wait in for neighbour's delivery

45

Birthday surprise backfired

Built a machine that turned against me

47

Had to win at Hide and Seek

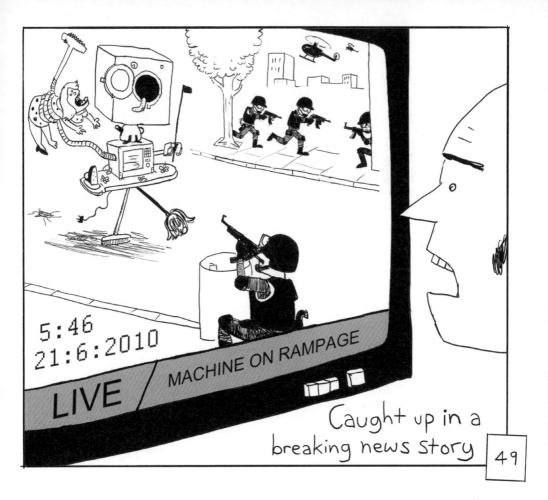

Caught up in a breaking news story

49

Had to identify a body

51

Shouldn't have bought a car online

Read something that upset me

Forgot to mind the gap

56

Stuck on hold

58

FLUOR-EX 2010

Determined to get the last out of the toothpaste

Flushed in a train station

59

Morning meditation went too well

Getting a useful tattoo

61

Held up giving directions

Getting to grips with my new phone

63

Testing my child for talent

Abducted by aliens

65

Abducted by other aliens

Subjected to a series of humiliating tests

67

My inner boy scout got the better of me

69

Last night's seafood came back to haunt me

Home hair transplant had unexpected side effects

71

Children possessed at breakfast

Attacked by brass rubbers

73

Got lost at a Where's Wally? Convention

WALLY BURGER

Suffered a porridge catastrophe

75

Became a YouTube phenomenon

77

A bad situation deteriorated

Got sued

79

Forgot to put away the crayons

Had a sudden attack of agoraphobia

81

Decided to try every coffee place on the way to work

Discovered I'm the star of a reality tv show

83

Waylaid by a caricaturist

Shouldn't have worn my bread hat

85

Parking dispute got out of hand

Accidentally launched escape pod

87

Failed to prepare for global warming

Left the cloning machine on all night

89

Had to call out a mechanic

91

Stumbled through a series of time portals

93

Team building weekend lasted longer than expected

Witnessed a miracle

97

Dog ate my miracle

Overslept

99

Realised lateness is a relative concept

Bit off more than I could chew

101